"

The R

Abdallah Saliou

We have a wrong concept of existence. Someone has painted a totally backwards and upside down picture of reality. We have been taught to look at the world through the eyes of someone who had no clue about the true nature of existence, Allah, and the reality of being.

I. The True Nature of Existence

Before creation, there was only Allah. Allah is now, as He was before creation. Allah is the only being in existence. Allah has said in the Holy Quran that he created the heavens and the earth in truth. Allah is the truth. Allah has said in one Hadith Qudsi, "I was a hidden treasure, and I wanted to be known. I created creation so that I might be known."

Allah created all that exists from His own essence. Allah did not use something other than Himself to create with, because at the time of creation, Allah was the only one in existence. Everyone knows that Allah is the First and the Last. We must come to realize that Allah is all that EXISTS between the First and the Last. Allah does not have or share any partners in His existence. Allah has said in the Holy Quran that there will come a time when all things will CEASE to exist, except for the face of Allah. Allah has also said in the Holy Quran that all things return to Him and that to Him is the journeying.

Allah is like an omnipresent ocean with no beginning or ending. All of creation and existence are like waves from this ocean, which can never be separated from the ocean. When we view creation, and that which exists on the physical PLANE, we have been taught to focus on the waves as individual entities in and of themselves, instead of focusing on the ocean and the unity of the source of existence of all the waves. When viewing an ocean, it is easy to see that all of the waves originate from and are connected to the ocean. When a wave goes down and becomes one with the ocean, it is impossible to tell the difference between the wave and the ocean. We are the waves. Allah is the ocean. We are waves from the Ocean.

I. ALLAH

Surah 112 of the Holy Quran. THE UNITY.

In the name of Allah the Beneficent and Merciful.

1. Say Allah is one.

2. Allah is Eternal and Absolute.

3. He begets not nor is He begotten.

4. There is none like Him, the One.

Allah is one. His oneness does not mean that He is one in the first of many. His oneness is Eternal, which means that there is no possibility of another existing after Him or with Him in existence. Allah is one without a second. Allah was NOT created. Allah has, does, and will always exist. WE MUST understand that Allah is not begotten and Allah does Not beget.

There is nothing like or comparable to Allah because Allah is the only one in existence without anything to compare Himself to.

LA-EE-LA-HA-ILL-ALLAH has an exoteric and an esoteric meaning. The exoteric, outer meaning, is that there is no God but ALLAH. ALLAH is that which exists, has being. The esoteric, inner meaning, is that there is no existence other than the existence of ALLAH.

I. The Reality of Being

To be or not to be, that is the question. Do we exist or do we not exist? Some schools of thought teach that we must develop a certain level of being to take with us and exist in the next life. This is a false idea. Being is that which has always existed and does not need to be developed. HOWEVER, we may become aware of or conscious of our true nature/being. This does not mean that at one time our being did not exist and needed to be developed.

The essence of the wave is not separate from the essence of of the ocean. The wave MAY have taken a form. This form is only temporary. A wave would be foolish to think that it has a separate existence because it can be measured by length, width, and height. Length, width, and height are only attributes of the physical world, which is temporary and not eternal. When a wave recognizes its true relationship with the ocean, it will realize that it had no real existence. The wave's existence is the existence of the ocean in a form that the ocean might know, and return to itself. Remember all waves return to the ocean and the ocean knows itself through the existence of the wave.

6

THE SUFI ON THE BUS

"A Journey to Knowledge of Self!"

Day 1 *** Overcoming Fear***

Day 2 ***Overcoming Anger***

Day 3 ***Overcoming Greed***

Day 4 ***Overcoming Lust***

Day 5 ***Overcoming the Ego***

Jihad-Ul Nafs (War Against the Lower Self)

The Sufi On The Bus

"A Jorney to Knowledge of Self"

Day 1 ***Overcoming Fear***

Early this morning a hostile person approached me on the bus. She asked me, "Are you going to kill everyone on the bus?" I responded, "Yes" with a hypothetical look, tone and voice. Why did she assume that from my outer appearance I was an Islamic Terrorist on a suicide mission? Actually, I was trying to kill myself (my lower self), but how could she have known this from the outer appearance of things unless she had been blessed with divine insight. Divine insight is the ability to look beyond the outer appearance of all things or situations to see Allah's divine reality beyond all material things and Allah's plan beyond the appearance of any situation. Fear is f-false e-evidence a-appearing r-real. We should not let outer appearances influence our inner emotional state, all outer appearances and things change with time!

Allah says in the Holy Qur'an, "there will come a time when all things fade away, and only the face of Allah will exist." Allah also says in the Holy Qur'an, "Wherever you turn there is the face of Allah." Fear is caused by a false knowledge of self. A false knowledge of self-causes one to think that the self was born, and one day the self will die. A person with true knowledge of self knows that the true self was never born, never dies and cannot be affected by the outer illusion, the world. A person with this level of knowledge knows that Allah is the only being in existence and that their being is not separate from His Being. The only reality that exists is Allah. Why should we fear outer appearances, "that are illusions cast On the screen of the mind", as one mystic says. The Holy Qur'an talks about a group of people who neither fear nor Grieve. On our journey to knowledge of self, we must try to Emulate these people and overcome fear that is caused by false Evidence appearing real and a false knowledge of self.

Day 2 Overcoming Anger***

Today on my way home there was a man and a woman arguing on the bus stop downtown. The man was angry about something that seemed to be of little or no importance to the woman. as he ranted and raved on about the situation, the woman paid him no attention. She sat there quietly waiting on the bus. Finally, the man yelled some obscenities and stomped off into the street not noticing the oncoming car. What was it that made this man so angry with the woman that he almost lost his life in a car accident? He had to be rushed to the hospital in an ambulance only because he was not paying attention to what he was doing when he stomped into the street. I will never know the answer to that question, but I do know that there are things that have happened to me in my life that made me so angry that I was not rational about my actions. The Prophet Muhammad, Peace Be Upon Him, has been noted to have said, "Do not get angry." Anger can cloud our judgment and rational thinking and causes us to be unaware of what we are doing. Anger is an unstable emotional state that can cause us to do things that we often regret. One way to control our anger is to pay attention to and control our breathing rate when involved in situations that may cause us to get angry. An angry person generally has a faster breathing rate than a calm person does. In situations that may cause us to get angry we should try to keep our breathing rate at a normal or even lower than normal level. This technique can prevent us from reaching a level of anger that may cause us to do something that we would later regret. On our journey to knowledge of self, we must overcome anger and uncontrolled actions associated with it.

Day 3 ***Overcoming Greed***

Today on the bus, on my way home, I saw five birds on the Side of the street eating a piece of bread. One of the birds snatched

The bread and quickly flew away leaving the other four birds with
Nothing to eat. Some people behave in the same manner as this one
Bird, taking or keeping material things for themselves without
Considering the needs of others. Allah says in the Holy Qur'an,
"woe to the worshippers who pray to be seen by others and refuse to
supply needs of their neighbors." This is caused by greed. Greed is
the desire for more of a thing that is actually needed by a person.
The level of greed is related to the focal point of the person's five
senses. If a person's five senses are focused on the outer world, their
desire for material objects will increase because of an attraction to
the outer world. If a person's five senses are focused on the inner
spiritual world, their desire for material objects will decrease because
of an attraction to more spiritual things. The focal point of a
person's five senses determines the focal point of a person's heart. If
a person's five senses are focused outward, then a person's heart
will be focused on the outer world and things of a material nature. If
a person's five senses are focused inward than a person's heart will

be focused on the inner world and things of a more spiritual nature. A person whose heart is filled with greed cannot be focused inwardly at the same time. A person whose heart is focused inwardly cannot be filled with greed at the same time. Allah says in the Holy Qur'an that for some people the life of this world is just for sport and play, and competition for the gain of material wealth. The Holy Qur'an also says that the next life is the real life and that at the time of death our eyesight will become clear. On our journey to knowledge of self there must come a time when our hearts are turned inwardly and greed is no longer a personal attribute that effects us.

Day 4 ***Overcoming Lust***

Today on the bus I saw two dogs in someone's front yard engaged in sexual intercourse. Seeing this event was not strange to me, but it caused me to think about the fact that dogs only have sex during mating seasons and for the production of offspring. During mating seasons dogs are said to be in "heat."

The

It occurred to me that for dogs the time for being in "heat" only last Part of each year. Why is it that we as humans may be in "heat" for An entire adult lifetime and not just for the production of offspring? We as humans are the highest creations of Allah, and a times we are at a lower level than some animals because of an uncontrolled sex drive. An uncontrolled sex drive is the result of lust. Humans have been said to have seven main spiritual centers that run from the base of the spine to the top of the head. The bottom three centers are related to the lower self and lower desires. The upper four centers starting from the heart center up to the head, crown center, are related to the higher self. A person's behavior is usually dictated by which spiritual center is open and dominant. A person whose behavior is motivated by lust is operating out of the second spiritual center, which is located by the genital area of the body. Fasting and decreasing the amount of meat you eat can help control lust.

Lust involves the focusing and usage of energy externally. When one is fasting energy is conserved and used internally. A diet that consists of eating large amounts of meat provides energy for then lower three spiritual centers. Allah asks the question in the Holy Qur'an, "Has there not come over man a long period of time when he Was nothing worth mentioning?" This can be said because of the lust That plaques the human race. On our journey to knowledge of self We must overcome this uncontrolled sex drive called "lust" and not Live on a lower level than animals.

Day 5 ***Overcoming the Ego***

Anyone who rides the bus knows that sometimes on the bus you will hear the conversations of others, not because you are eaves dropping, but because of those close seating on the bus as well as the fact that people often times do not talk discreetly on the bus. On the bus today I heard a man say that he was superior because he was black, and that his melanin made him superior to other people, whom he said, did not have any melanin. This man based his theory of being superior on physical characteristics.

In the Holy Qur'an the devil was cast out of heaven for not bowing Down to the Prophet Adam, peace be upon him. The devil said that He was superior to Adam (P.B.U.H.) because Allah had created him From smokeless fire, and Adam (P.B.U.H.) was only created Fro sounding clay. In this story the devil based his feeling of superiority on physical characteristics. Feeling of superiority over others because of physical characteristics, is caused by the ego. Man is composed of two natures, one physical and one spiritual. These two natures are often called the lower self and the higher self. The ego is an attribute of the physical nature, the lower self. If a person feels that they are better than others are, then they feel good about themselves. And therefore, the ego, their false sense of individuality, feels safe and protected. The ego represents a false sense of self, and must be overcome on our journey to knowledge of self. The Prophet Muhammad (P.B.U.H.) has been noted to have said, "Die before you Die." This eludes the death of the ego, false sense of individuality, which must die in order for true spiritual development to take place. In Islam a war is called a jihad. In order for the ego to die, an internal war must be fought. This internal war that must be fought is known in Arabic as the jihad-ul nafs (war against the lower self).

Jihad-Ul Nafs (War Against the Lower Self)

After one of the wars during the lifetime of Prophet Muhammad (P.B.U.H.) the Prophet told his companions, on their Way home, that they were leaving the minor war and going to the Major war. When asked what the major war was, the Prophet said That the major war was the jihad-ul nafs (war against the lower self). The beginning of the conscious practice of Islam for a person starts With the shahadah, testament of faith. The beginning of victory over the lower self starts with the acceptance of true Cheikh. This does not mean that everyone who accepts a Cheikh as their teacher will defeat the lower self; it simply means that the chances for success are greatly improved. The war against the lower self involves the defeating of man's avowed enemy, the devil. The devil is a jinn that has so much knowledge that at one time he used to teach the angels in heaven.

When the devil was cast out of heaven he asked Allah for permission To test man. He was given permission to test man until the Day of Judgment. For us to think that we can defeat the devil, with the Knowledge we have learned from reading some books is an illusion. That is why we need the guidance of a true Cheikh. A true Cheikh is One who has defeated the devil and their lower self. The pledge that is taken with a Cheikh is known in Arabic as a bayat. In the Holy Qur'an some of the companions of the Prophet Muhammad (P.B.U.H.) took bayat with him under a tree. The name of the surah in which this event is found is Fatah. In English Fatah has been translated to mean victory. In surah Fatah, the victory, Allah says in verse tens, "surely those who swear allegiance to you do but swear allegiance to Allah; the hand of Allah is above their hands." In verse 18 in the same surah, Allah says, "certainly Allah was well pleased with the believers when they swore allegiance to you under the tree, and He knew what was in their hearts. So, He sent down tranquility on them and rewarded them with a near victory." In this chapter of the Holy Qur'an, The Victory, Allah associates victory with the bayat. Allah also says that He was pleased with the believers when they swore their allegiance. On our journey to knowledge of self, we must all seek a true Cheikh to take bayat with to receive Allah's pleasure, and a near victory of the lower self.

THOUGHTS MANIFEST

THE SUBSTANCE OF THINGS UNSEEN

THE PRECURSOR FOR ALL PHYSICLE BEINGS

THOUGHTS VISIONS AND DREAMS

FORM THREE DIMINSIONAL THINGS

IN THE BEGINNING WAS THE WORD

THIS WORD WAS IN THE MIND

ON EARTH AS IT IS IN HEAVEN

THOUGHTS MANIFEST WITH THE PASSAGE OF TIME

THOUGHTS ARE THE SEEDS THAT WE CAST INTO THE GROUND

PRAYER IS FOCUSED THOUGHT INSIDE THE SILENCE OF SOUND

WORDS ARE VIBRATIONS

VIBRATION IS PART OF CREATION

ALLAH SPEAKS THINGS INTO EXISTANCE

THOUGHTS MANIFEST WITH MENTAL PERSISTANCE

THOUGHTS MANIFEST

A.S.

<u>786</u>

WALKING ON THIS PATH SOMETIMES IS HECTIC
UPHILL
TRIALS SHOULD BE EXPECTED
TURN BACK, TURN BACK THE HANDS OF TIME
MIND OVER MATER, MEDIATE TO STILL THE MIND
ILLUSION CLOUD PERCEPTION
QUESTION
ARE YOU IN THE RIGHT DIRECTION?
DEATH IS A BRIDGE THAT MUST BE CROSSED
STUDY THE SIGNS NOW SO YOU WON'T BE LOST
THE SPIRIT PLANE
VIBRATES FASTER
KUNDALINI SHOULD ONLY BE RAISED BY A MASTER
LIFE IS A GAME SIMILAR TO CHESS
STEP AWAY FROM THE GAME AND YOU CAN SEE IT BEST
TAI CHI, MANTRA, DUALITY, YIN YANG
EASTERN PHILOSOPHY, SUFI, I CHING
RETURN OF THE JEDI, OPENING OF THE 3RD . EYE
DIE B-4 U DIE AND BECOME IMORTAL
THE EGYPTIAN MYSTERIES HAVE BEEN REVEALED
THIS IS THE TURNING OF THE SEVENTH WHEEL
HIDDEN WISDOM FOR THE MASSES IN AQUARIUS
RISE UP SANKOFA
THE PHENIX WILL FLY AGAIN
WE ARE EXPEIENCING TOTAL RECALL
OF HIGHER PLANES OF EXISTENCE BEFORE THE FALL
THE MATRIX IS REAL
THIS IS A HOLOGRAPHIC UNIVERSE
THE THEORY OF RELATIVITY MUST BE REVERSED
LIGHT UPON LIGHT
EXPERIENCE THE TRANSMISSION
WHAT WILL IT TAKE TO END THIS CONDITION   A.S.

Bus

THE ULTIMATE REALITY

THE CIRCLE WITH THE CIRCLE
THE REALITY BEYOND THE ILLUSION.
YES. THIS REALM ONLY EXISTS ON THE PLANE OF THE MIND.
WHAT DID YOU FIND?
THE MAZE HAS ONLY ONE EXIT.
CERTAIN TRUTHS MUST BE ACCEPTED.
THE WISE ATHIEST PROVES TO BE A FOOL.
WHEN THEY PHILOSOPHICALLY TRY TO REJECT IT.
HOW CAN YOU USE THE MIND TO DISPROVE THAT WHICH IS BEYOND
THE MIND.
HOW CAN YOU USE TIME TO MEASURE THAT WHICH IS BEYOND TIME
OPEN YOUR HEART, OPEN YOUR HEART
THE HEART MUST BE OPEN
TO EXPERIENCE THE ULTIMATE REALITY.
TO EXPERIENCE IS TO KNOW
TO KNOW IS TO GLOW TO GLOW IS TO SHOW
LIGHT ONLY EXISTS
WALK IN THE LIGHT WITH THE LIGHT BECOME LIGHT
THAT YOU WERE BEFORE BIRTH
AFTER THE DEATH OF THE EGO
LET ME EGGO OR EGO
I DIE DAILY I DIE DAILY I DIE DAILY
THE INDIVIDUAL I MUST DIE
THAT THE ULTIMATE REALITY MIGHT EXPRESS THROUGH ME
AS ME BECOME ME
NOT THE ME THAT YOU SEE
BUT THE ME THAT MUST BE
THE ULTIMATE REALITY
THE ULTIMATE REALITY ON ALL PLAINS EXISTENCE
ETERNAL EXISTENCE
THIS WORLD IS JUST A MEAR SHADOW
THAT RELFECTS A BEING THAT IS
TIMELESS DEATHLESS PEERLESS
HAVING NO EQUAL
NO PART TWO NO SEQUAL
REALISE THAT THE ONE WE ARE SEEKING
SHOULD ONLY BE SOUGHT INSIDE OF SELF
WHAT IS THE REALITY BEYOND THE PROJECTED IMAGE IN THE
MIRROR. **THE ULTIMATE REALITY** A.S.

THE PURPOSE OF LIFE

THE MAJORITY OF PEOPLE ON THE PLANET EARTH WILL GO THROUGH LIFE AND NEVER EXPERIENCE AND KNOW THE REALITY OF THEIR BEING, AND ALLAH. THEY WILL PASS THROUGH THIS EXISTENCE AND MEASURE THEIR SUCCESS, OR GREATNESS BASED ON THE TRANSITORY THINGS OF AND ENDS WITH DEATH. BIRTH AND DEATH ARE TWO POINTS ON THE CIRCLE OF LIFE THAT IS ETERNAL. WE SHOULD NOT SPEND ALL OF OUR TIME FOCUSING ON THE (TIME?) BETWEEN THESE TWO POINTS. YES THIS (TIME?) IS IMPORTANT BECAUSE IT WILL DETERMINE OUR STATE WHEN WE PASS THROUGH THE DOOR OF LIFE CALLED DEATH.

IN LIFE IS DEATH. IN DEATH IS LIFE. WE ARE ETERNAL BEINGS THAT EXISTED BEFORE BIRTH AND WILL CONTINUE TO EXIST AFTER DEATH. WHEN WE STARTED STUDYING KNOWLEDGE OF SELF OUR FATHER ONCE ASKED US TO TRY AND FIGURE OUT WHERE WE WERE BEFORE BIRTH AND WHERE WE WOULD BE AFTER DEATH. IT HAS BEEN SAID THAT WHEN ANCIENT SUFIS WOULD MEET THEY WOULD ASK EACH OTHER WHERE DID YOU COME FROM, WHERE ARE YOU NOW, AND WHERE ARE YOU GOING? THE ANSWER TO THEIR ANCIENT QUESTIONS IS THE ANSWER TO OUR FATHERS QUESTION. WE CAME FROM ALLAH, WE ARE WITH ALLAH, AND WE ARE GOING TO ALLAH.

TO COME FROM SOMETHING, TO BE WITH SOMETHING, AND TO GO TO SOMETHING IMPLIES THE EXISTENCE OF TWO SEPARATE ENTITIES. ISLAM IS BASED ON ONENENESS. ALLAH IS ONE. ALLAH IS SELF-EXISTENCNT. ALLAH IS WITH ALLAH. ALLAH IS GOING TO ALLAH. WE AS INDIVIDUALS HAVE NOT INDEPENDENT EXISTENCE APART FROM ALLAH. WE HAVE BEEN TAUGHT THAT WE ARE HMAN BEINGS. "HU" IS AN ARABIC PRONOUN THAT MEANS ALLAH WITHOUT ANY GENDER ASSOCIATION. MAN MEANSE CONSCIOUSNESS. BEING MEANS TO EXIST. THUS THE WORD HU-MAN BEING MEANS ALLAH CONSCIOUSLY EXISTING. ALL THINGS EXIST IN ONENESS WITH ALLAH. WE ARE THE ONLY CREATIONS OF ALLAH THAT HAVE THE POTENTIAL TO BECOME CONSICOUS OF OUR ONENESS WITH ALLAH. THIS IS THE PURPOSE OF LIFE.

A.S.

MISSING PAGES OF ISLAM
KNOWLEDGE OF SELF & SUFISM

KNOWLEDGE OF SELF

What is self? False personalities? There is a world wide mass hypnosis taking place. We are suffering from the effects of the colonization of the mind. We have been given false ideas about the self by society. We have been trained to see our selves from a false view point. We have false ideas concerning the self. False ideas about the nature of reality.

The concepts of birth and death are false. The concept of Having a life span is false. There is no such thing as a birth and a Death as we have been taught. These are all false because any Concepts related to birth or death and a life span that starts with a Certain beginning and has a certain ending are false. As soon as we start to think that I was born, I'm living my life, and one day I will die, we start basing our reality off on these false ideas.

My father once said to me "what you need to figure out is Where were you before you were born, and where will you be after death, that is what is important." He referred to an aspect of the self that is before birth and that is going to continue on after death and it does not have anything to do with this in-between period (life span). There is something here in all of us that was not born, does not have a life span and does not die. Any time that we refer to ourselves as an African American, black, white, or anything referring to physical characteristics this is all false because the true self, who we really are, is beyond birth, beyond death and beyond a life span. It is beyond any aspect of duality. The true self is eternal with no beginning and no ending.

We have to get in tune with this true self and not this false self that we are accustomed to. People say "This is me, this is my hand, my face, my body," this is not you. This is the house you live in. At the time of what people call death the true self will leave this body behind like a pair of old clothes. In the bible it says "The body is the temple of God." One thing we have is a false sense of who we are. The true self is not born and does not die. This is something we have come to know and understand. We exist on three planes: physical, soul, and spirit. The spirit plane is light. The soul plane is light. The physical plane is light. Scientist have proven that the elements that make up the physical world (protons, neutrons and electrons) and all matter consist of particles of light that vibrate at a constant rate. What we call the physical realm is nothing but light.

Our eyes have been trained and our mind has been taught to Focus on the physical world as being solid. This realm is light Slowed down to vibrate at a constant rate. All of the atoms on this Plane of existence spin at the exact speed. This physical plane Is light that vibrates slower than the plane of soul, which is light That vibrates slower than the plane of spirit which is light. This is Light upon light. In the Holy Qur'an Allah talks about light upon Light in one of the most quoted verses by the Sufis. This is one of the missing pages of Islam that is not often talked about out side of the sufi community. This creation is all light. Allah is light. Allah has said in the Holy Qur'an that He is the light of the heavens and the earth and all that is in between. Allah said that we were created from one perfect spirit, and that He breathed His soul into us. The essence of the soul and spirit are one with Allah. The physical plane is where the confusion starts. When the soul is encased in the body, the soul starts to think that it is physical. It starts to identify with the physical world.

We are trained in this society to focus our five sense outward on the physical world. Because we are not taught to focus inward on the soul and spirit we start to think that we are physical beings. The true self is soul and spirit, one with Allah. There are three levels of development for the soul mentioned in the Qur'an: the animalistic, self accusing, and soul at peace. Allah says in the Qur'an "he indeed succeeds who purifies it." It refers to the soul. The soul must be purified of its animalistic characteristics in order to manifest the light of Allah. The person who does not undergo self purification is living on the same level as animals.

What do animals do? Animals base there lives on three basic things: procreation, recreation and habitation. Animals have offspring, play, and seek to have some type of nest, shelter, or dwelling place. Some animals even have jobs that they perform in their animal societies ie the worker ant. If our life consists of nothing other than these activities, we are living on the same level as animals.

There comes a point in time in the development of the soul when it will begin to question itself regarding its actions. It is at this point that the soul will start the process of self analysis, and develop to the level of the self accusing soul. The self accusing soul seeks for the higher purpose of life. It begins to question its origin. It begins to question the nature of its actions, are they based on righteousness or, are they self serving. The soul as this point has the chance to answer the call of the Light, or it can choose to stay in darkness. If the soul answers the call of the Light it can complete the process of self purification and become the soul at peace.

When the soul reaches the level of the soul at peace, it is not attracted to the glitter and show of this world. It knows that there is a Reality beyond this third dimension, and sets its focus on this Reality. Reaching the level of the soul at peace is not the end of the spiritual journey. It is from this point that we may begin to travel into the reality of Allah's oneness. This journey is endless!!!!!!!!!

When you have a dream where are you? It looks real? The prophet Muhammad said that we are all asleep, and that at the time of death we will awaken. Dreams are a key into the knowledge of self. The level of development of the soul is often shown in the dream of the seeker. Dreams on the animalistic level often depict the level of the animalistic soul. Dreams of a more spiritual nature often depict the spiritual development, and purification of the soul. Dreams can also be a window into the subconscious mind of the seeker. There are three sources for the origin of dreams: repressed desires from the world, a negative spiritual source, a positive spiritual source. Determining the origin of the dream can help determine the spiritual nature and usefulness of the dream.

In the Holy Qur'an Allah says that He takes the soul unto Himself When we sleep, and that He returns the soul to use when we awaken. The soul is the interface between the pure light realm, the spirit, and the slowed down realm of light, the physical plane. If your soul is more inclined towards the physical plane you will not be able to progress towards the Light. If your soul starts the process of purification, and is able to escape the false gravity of this world, it may realize its oneneness with the Light.

One of the popular sayings of the prophet Muhammad is the marriage is 50% of Islam. Some people would say that this marriage is the marriage between husband and wife. One inner meaning of this marriage is the merging of the soul and spirit of the seeker. It is when your soul and spirit become one. When the soul and the spirit have returned to oneness we will have returned to our original level of existence before the fall of man.

After we know who we are we need some kind of science, teaching, that will enable us to realize, and manifest our true nature.

Once we know that the true self is one with Allah we must start the Process of self realization. In the book <u>Waves from the Ocean</u> the author says "Allah is like an ocean and we are waves from the ocean." We are waves from the ocean of Allah's oneness. It would be foolish for a wave to ever think that it was separate from the ocean. Waves rise up and go down. When it rises up (birth) it looks like a wave but when it goes down (submission/Islam) it merges with the ocean.

There is no reality but the reality. There is no God but God. God is that which has being, that which exists. The only one that exists is the ocean. The only one that exists is Allah. Allah said "I was a hidden treasure and I wanted to be known, I created this realm so that I might be known." Allah created this creation so that He might be known. It is through the existence of the wave that the ocean knows itself. It is through the existence of this realm that Allah will know Allah. The aspect of the self has the ability to know Allah is Allah. Nothing can know Allah but Allah. Allah is beyond everything. The only being that can know Allah is Allah, Who is all knowing and omnipresent. Allah says in the Holy Qur'an that there will come a time when all existence will perish, and only the face of Allah will exits. We know this realm is temporary. Allah says in the Holy Qur'an. "Everywhere you look is the face of Allah." We are actually deceived by this realm. This world is actually not a mask covering Allah. What we are actually seeing is Allah's oneness but our mind cannot perceive this oneness because Allah hides Himself with Himself. There is nothing greater than Allah that could hide Allah's Oneness.

Prophet Muhammad said that he knows his Lord by his Lord. The prophet has also said "He who knows himself knows his Lord." If you know your true self then you will know Allah. If you know your self then you will have knowledge of Allah. That which will know Allah is actually Allah knowing Himself. The science, teaching, that can help us to know and manifest the true potential of the self is Sufism.

Sufism

There are two sides two every coin. Everything has an inner and an outer meaning. The inner side of Islam is Sufism. Sufism is the process by which we are able to realize our nothingness, and Allah's oneness. Islam is a way of life that has four main branches of knowledge: shariat, tariqat, haqiqat, and marifat.

The shariat is based on five pillars: testimony of faith, prayer, charity, fasting, and pilgrimage. The beginning of the shariat is the testimony of faith, there is none worthy of worship but God, and Muhammad is the prophet of God. The shariat also consists of the religious laws of Islam. The shariat is one and is practiced by all muslims.

The tariqat is the inner pathway that leads to knowledge of Allah's oneness. The beginning of the tariqat is the acceptance of a cheikh, teacher. The cheikh is the spiritual guide along the path, having traveled the path himself, he knows all of the pitfalls of the path. The cheikh hold the keys that will unlock the spiritual potential this is latent within
the seeker.

The haqiqat is the truth of reality. The beginning of the realization of haqiqat starts when the individual "I" of the seeker starts to disappear and the universal, non-personal "I" begins to manifest through the seeker. The essence of haqiqat is the realization that only Allah exists, and that we as individuals have no true existence separate from the omnipresent existence of Allah.

Marifat is knowledge of Allah, gnosis. This knowledge has no beginning and no ending. The knowledge of Allah is revealed to the arif (knower) stage by stage. Marifat is the state of being absent from creation, and present with the Creator. The prophet Muhammad said that there are seventy thousand veils of light between Allah and the seeker. Marifat is knowledge of Allah that is obtained from the removal of these veils.

Example: I have heard that there is a fire in the forest (shariat). I begin to travel to the fire in the forest (tariqat). I am burned and totally consumed by the fire (haqiqat). I start to know, and understand the nature of the fire (marifat). This is the life, goal, and pathway of the sufi. Death before death, "die before you die", the false self must dies so that we might know Allah, and the essence of the true self.

Made in the USA
Columbia, SC
03 December 2023